A REPRINT OF A RARE BOOKLET BY TRACY R. TWYMAN FROM *DAGOBERT'S REVENGE MAGAZINE* PUBLICATION ERA

[B&W ON 70LB PAPER, SIZE 5.5"X8.5"]

THE RULE OF THE IRON SCEPTER (THE APOCALYPSE PLOT), IS A 13-14 PAGES BOOKLET ESSAY WRITTEN IN 2001 FOR *DAGOBERT'S REVENGE MAGAZINE*. POSSIBLY A SUPPLEMENTARY MATERIAL THAT CAME WITH AN ISSUE OF THE MAGAZINE.

THE RULE OF THE IRON SCEPTER,
ALSO KNOWN AS
THE APOCALYPSE PLOT

ISBN 978-1-962312-21-9

MYSTAGOGUE PUBLICATIONS
2001 & 2023

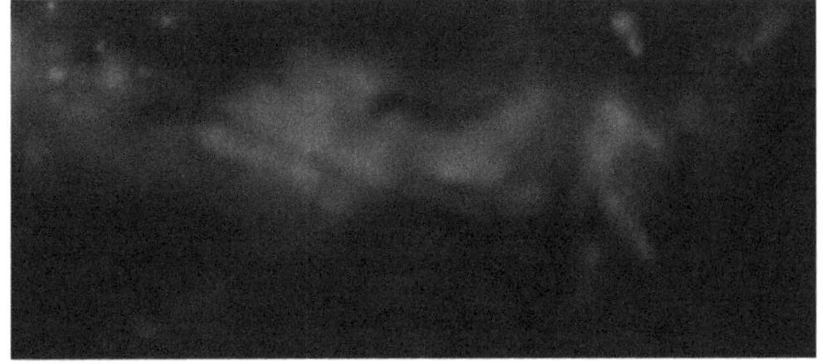

The Rule of the Iron Scepter

Also Known As

The Apocalypse Plot

Dagobert's Revenge
PO BOX 18331
DENVER, CO 80218-0331
USA

www.dagobertsrevenge.com

The Rule of the Iron Scepter

Also Known As

The Apocalypse Plot

by Tracy R. Twyman, E.G.M.

With the safe passage of the year 2000, prophesized by many to be the beginning of the Great Tribulation, many religious people breathed a sigh of relief, and returned to their care-free, sinful lives. Those who had saved up supplies and provisions in preparation for the predicted catastrophe tore into them almost as soon as Dec. 31, 1999 had passed. After all, there seemed to be no need for them. The Western world was at peace, the economy was great, and all of the computers that supported the economy were working perfectly. Many derided those who had expected a Doomsday scenario, those superstitious, radical "fundamentalists" who foolishly awaited the rise of the Anti-Christ, and his defeat by the Second Coming of Christ. Some even haughtily proclaimed a New Age of peace and prosperity, a time of Goddess-worship, free love, and the copious use of various "essential oils."

Then came the events of September 11, 2001, and the revelry abruptly screeched to a halt. With the first year of the new millennium barely half-way through, a realization sunk in that a new age was indeed being ushered in, but not some tie-dyed, hippy-dippy love-fest. Nay, the Angel of Death hath descended upon the land, and few with any knowledge of the scriptures would hesitate to say that the End Times are at hand. The old order is most certainly finished, and we are its last generation.

Many cultures have predicted a bloody apocalypse at the end of time, from the Ragnarok of Nordic peoples to the end of the Mayan calendar, which will occur a mere 11 years from now. The prediction of wars, earthquakes, floods, and pestilences is almost universal, often accompanied by the return of that culture's father-god, who will establish a new order, and reign directly over his people once again for thousands of years, as he has in the distant past. For as universal as the tale of an upcoming Armageddon is, so too are the traditions of past apocalypses, worldwide calamities that destroyed previous civilizations, bringing an end to the Golden Age when the gods ruled directly over man upon the Earth. The impression one gets is of a recurring cycle of apocalypses, a ritual cleansing of the world caused by cyclical pole shifts and planetary collisions, but also caused, spiritually, by the sins of mankind.

The Judeo-Christian version of the Apocalypse is no exception. A brief look at *The Revelation of St. John the Divine* shows that it bears strong resemblances to the apocalyptic histories of other cultures, things that those cultures say have already happened, and which the archeological record attests to. The sun becomes black, the moon red as blood. A fiery mountain is cast into the sea, and a star called "Wormwood" falls into the Earth, poisoning the waters thereof. "And the heaven departed as a scroll when it is rolled together; and every mountain and island moved out of their places." (Rev. 5:14) This matches almost precisely the stories of the destruction of Atlantis as described by Plato, and the Flood of Noah described in *Genesis* and *The Book of Enoch*, events that occurred in the distant past, but are described in *Revelation* as chronologically preceding the rule of the Anti-Christ. But one would assume that after the events just described, there would be no kingdom left for him to rule over, certainly not one as grand and glorious as Babylon the Great. Perhaps St. John was merely seeing visions of the past, to prepare him for the visions he was about to have of the future. Perhaps part of what he was meant to see and realize was that this is a cycle, in which God repeatedly creates mankind, rules directly over him, and then abandons him,

allows him to spread wickedness over the Earth for millennia. At some point, finally, he destroys him, and rules over the few, righteous remnants again in a "Second Coming" of the "Kingdom of God" - over, and over, and over again. One thing we can all be sure of about our deities is their love of ritual, and the Apocalypse ritual is certainly one of their most sacred, a ceremonial sacrifice of their greatest creation, mankind, which they apparently repeat every few thousand years.

Of all the apocalypse scenarios from various cultures, the Judeo-Christian one is by far the most specific in terms of predicting what religio-political events will lead up to the calamity. For prior to the return of the "King of Kings", Jesus Christ, the Bible tells us that the majority of the Earth's population will unite under a single monarch, the spawn of the Devil himself, the Anti-Christ. He will rule foremostly over a kingdom depicted in *Revelation* as taking the symbolic form of a dragon, "with seven heads and ten horns, and upon his horns ten crowns, and upon his heads the name of blasphemy." (*Rev.* 13: 1) This is the same beast that is described earlier in Chapter 12 as having been cast out of Heaven. "And his tail drew a third part of the stars of Heaven, and did cast them to the Earth." (*Rev.*12:4) This is, of course, the same story as the Biblical "War in Heaven", in which Lucifer, God's most beloved angel (and according to Jewish apocryphal tradition, God's first-born son) was cast out of Heaven for his rebellious nature, along with a third of the other angels, who had decided to rebel with him. This is represented in the Old Testament as chronologically preceding the Flood, and indeed, the whole event sounds like a mythologized account of a celestial occurrence, one that probably accompanied a catastrophic polar shift. The "Dragon" is Draco, a constellation that encircles the whole of the night's sky, and is depicted as swallowing his own tail. A polar shift caused it to appear, from the perspective of ancient man, that he, along with one-third of the stars, had been cast out of the sky and into the sea - the sea that the Dragon would eventually rise out of again at the End of Time. This beast became thereafter known as Leviathan, "the Dragon of the Deep", and the ocean itself, known also as "the Abyss", was thereafter associated with him.

Many Bible prophecy preachers today are quite certain that the Beast of Revelation represents the rising European Union, which is quickly coalescing from an economic partnership into a true political empire of nations, a process that has been greatly facilitated by the events of September 11. Many see in this union a revitalization of the old Holy Roman Empire, held together in the Middle Ages by the Roman Catholic Church, as well as other Vatican-approved monarchs. Most of these monarchs, as well as their supreme head, the Holy Roman Emperor himself, came from royal houses which descended from the family that first held the title "New Constantine", a prototype of the Holy Roman Emperor title. That family was the Frankish line of the Merovingians, a line that most modern European royals, as well as all 44 of the U.S. presidents, are descendants of. As many of our readers know, the Merovingians, including their modern-day descendants, consider themselves to be inheritors of the blood lineage of Jesus Christ himself, through his consort, Mary Magdalen.

As the story goes, Christ survived the crucifixion, and fled with his pregnant wife to the Jew-friendly area of Southern France, where a substantial number of his kinsmen were already settled. There his descendants intermarried with local Visigothic nobility, giving birth to the royal line that would provide Europe with all of its subsequent monarchs, as well as the heads of the Holy Roman Empire. That makes these people not only descendants of Christ, but also of the Judaic King David. Indeed, the royalty of Europe mimic the royalty of ancient Israel in form, symbol and ceremony very closely, cherishing their Davidic heritage as the source of their "Divine Right" to rule. For the throne of David was installed by God himself, who decreed that the office would be passed down to David's descendants until the end of time. "The sceptre shall not depart from Judah... until Shiloh come." (*Gen.* 49: 10)

Perhaps this is why our Anglo-European culture, presumed by most to be made up of Gentiles with pagan ancestry, is the world's main proponent and bastion of *Judeo*-Christian theology. In fact, many, such as Herbert W. Armstrong of the Worldwide Church of God, believe that it is not just our political leaders, but the majority of our population that carries the blood of the Israelites. Armstrong maintains that the ten "lost tribes of Israel" are in fact to be found today scattered across Europe, Britain, and the colonies like the U.S. , Canada, and Australia. He makes a convincing case by analyzing words and place-names found throughout Europe that appear to be based in Hebrew. He argues that the word "brit" comes from "berith", the Hebrew word for "covenant", and that the word "Saxons" (as in "Anglo-Saxons") comes from "Issac's Son's." He also points out a number of locations throughout Europe and especially Ireland that could have been named after the tribe of Dan, such as "Dundalk", "Dundee, "Donegal", and of course, "Denmark", meaning "Dan's Mark." He also points to historical Irish legends stating that sometime prior to 700 B.C., a tribe called the "Tuatha de Dannan" (Tribe of Dan) arrived on the coast of Ireland and settled down, driving out other tribes along the way. He then recounts a rather significant Irish legend regarding a supposed visit by the Prophet Jeremiah in 569 B.C. In that year "an elderly, white-haired patriarch", whom the locals referred to as a "saint" came to Ireland with a young woman named "Tea-Telphi", who was the daughter of an Egyptian king, and her husband, "Simon Brach." Simon was the son of the King of Ireland, and the two had met in Jerusalem, shortly before the siege. They then went back to Ireland, along with Jeremiah, bearing a harp, an ark, and something called the "lia-fail", which later became known as the "Stone of Destiny", the stone upon which all British monarchs must sit at their coronation. This is the same one that the Brits believe to be synonymous with Jacob's fabled pillow-stone, upon which he slept as he dreamt about wrestling with an angel. Armstrong finds significance in the fact that the word "lia-fail" reads the same forwards and backwards, perhaps an indication of it's Hebraic origin.

It is the tribe of Dan that is named by many Bible prophecy preachers as being the tribe from which the Anti-Christ will spring. For one thing, Dan is the only tribe not mentioned in *Revelation* as having been "sealed" on their foreheads as "Children of God." One must assume, then, that the Danites are "sealed" with that other mark, the number of the Beast, 666. Furthermore, as J.R. Church writes in *The Guardians of the Grail*, "Four symbols are used in the Bible regarding the Danites - a serpent, an eagle, a lion, and the bees." The first three are symbols now commonly used in European heraldry by Merovingian descendants, the serpent often being depicted as a dragon. The bees, however, are a symbol quite specific to the Merovingian dynasty. Church continues: "In the story of Samson [who was a Danite], we find the famous riddle of the bees who made honey in the carcass of a lion, which had been killed by Samson. The symbolic nature of the bees could represent the concept that the descendants of the tribe of Dan would one day try to bring about the destruction of Judah, whose symbol was the lion, and from the carcass of the lion the tribe of Dan would attempt to produce the golden age of a world empire, symbolized by the honey." Samson is further connected symbolically to the Merovingians because he, like the Merovingian kings, had hair with magical powers that disappeared when it was shorn. As for the serpent symbolism, this is supposedly based on the association of Dan with the astrological sign of Scorpio, although a scorpion is, in this author's estimation, not quite a serpent. The Priory of Sion, the modern organization dedicated to the propagation of Merovingian interests, has published a poem with the suggestive title of *Le Serpent Rouge* - "The Red Serpent." It contains 13 stanzas, each written for a different sign of the zodiac, with a thirteenth sign called "Ophiucus - The Serpent Holder", inserted *after* Scorpio and before Sagittarius. Perhaps, in addition to referring to the red dragon of *Revelation*, this poem alludes to a thirteenth sign that is the real zodiac house of Dan, and perhaps also a thirteenth tribe of Israel that has been hidden from the public record. Dan is also associated with the serpent because of *Genesis* 49:17, which states: "Dan will be a serpent by the roadside, a viper along the path, that bites the horse's heels." But perhaps the tribe of Dan wished to do more than merely destroy the lion of Judah. It seems as likely that Dan wished to unite with Judah, to intermarry into his bloodline and rightfully assume his God-given throne. After all, both tribes are referred to in Genesis as "a lion's whelp", perhaps indicating a connection between the two. And author Harold Camping has suggested that, "The king to come, the Messiah, will be of the House of David (Judean), but his mother will be a Danite." Does this refer to the fact that David's consort, Bathsheeba, was a Danite? Or to a more recent union of the tribes in the form of the Merovingian bloodline?

More evidence for a Danite origin of the Merovingians lies in the fact that Meroveus, the founder of the dynasty, is traditionally a descendant of Odin, linguistically connected with Dan, and that the Merovingians claims descent from the royal house of Troy, which was founded by Dar*dan*os, son of Zeus, a figure we have associated with the Biblical figure of Cain, and with the origins of the Tuatha de Danaan. The tales of the Tuatha de Danaan have a mythic quality about them, and match almost precisely those of the Nephilim, the fallen angels who according to the Bible, and to other ancient legends, intermarried with mortal women to create a bloodline of kings that comingled mortal genes with divine ones. This was, according to tradition, the cause of the War in Heaven in which Lucifer was cast to Earth. Among the offspring of this human-angel union was Cain, who was, say the legends, the son of Eve by Lucifer himself. Cain went on to become the father of a race of giants, called Cainites or Canaanites, who built civilizations all over the world. Cain himself founded a number of cities himself, and we have argued that he is essentially synonymous with Nimrod, who built the Tower of Babel. Although the race of Cain is popularly thought to have been cursed by God, the Bible says that God placed a mark upon Cain and all his descendants cursing those who would do *them* harm, even after the murder of his brother, Abel. In fact, the Cainites are remembered by every other culture as magnificent kings - teachers of wisdom, builders of nations. Even the word "king" comes from "Cain." He was worshipped by his people as a god, depicted in the form of a sea-bull, or a "dragon." This was the Babylonian religion that the Hebrews found so idolatrous and offensive. It even included the sacrifice of babies in a fiery pit. And yet many of the Hebrews, including their kings, practiced this religion, and intermarried with Canaanite women. Thus it is conceivable, if not certain, that the bloodline of Cain interbred with the Davidic bloodline that eventually resulted in Jesus. The Merovingian Franks alluded to their Cainite descent with their legend that their founder, Meroveus, was the spawn of a sea-bull called the "Quinotaur", a word not to be found in any dictionary, but which is etymologically linked with the name of Cain. Perhaps it is this intermingling of holy and infernal bloodlines that the Merovingian descendants the Angevins were referring to with their use of the double-barred Cross of Lorraine, said to represent both the blood of Christ, and of Satan, "the same artery and the same vein."

Interestingly, the worship of Jesus as God incarnate has lead to the formation of a religion that is, in all outward forms, a resurrection of the old Babylonian religion of Cain. Many of the ceremonies, including Mass, Communion, Baptism, and Confession, are taken directly from the Babylonian priesthood, as well as many of the symbols and idols used by Catholicism. The construction of the Cathedrals resembles the ancient pagan temples of Babylon, and even the structure of the priesthood is the same, along with the requirements of celibacy and wearing black. But most importantly, the deities are, at heart, the same. All of the saints are said to possess powers that correspond with those of various pagan deities, and are worshipped as such by many people, especially throughout the third world. The familiar statues of Mother Mary holding the baby Jesus mimic precisely those of Babylon's Ishtar holding her baby. She, like the Virgin Mary, was called the "Queen of Heaven", and the "Mother of God." The traditional Catholic depiction of Mary ascending to Heaven matches that of the Babylonian goddess in every detail. This depiction is also precisely described in the 12th Chapter of *Revelation*: "And there appeared a great wonder in heaven, a woman clothed with the sun, and the moon under her feet, and upon her head a crown of 12 stars." This woman gives birth to, "a man child, who was to rule all nations with a rod of iron." This person is either the Anti-Christ, or his ancestor, Cain. Both would match this description.

The seven-headed dragon, as we know, is Europe. But what of the "Scarlet Whore" referred to in *Revelation* as riding on the back of the Great Beast, the one called "Mystery, Babylon the Great, Mother of Harlots and Abominations of the Earth"? There can be little doubt that Rome is the scarlet whore. This is made clear when it is specifically stated that, "The seven heads [of the Beast] are the seven mountains on which the woman sitteth." (*Rev.* 17:9) Rome was built upon seven hills. The ten crowns represent the ten kings who will be in charge of the European Union, presumably descendants of the ten lost tribes of Israel. The scarlet woman is also said in *Revelation* to be in possession of, "a golden cup in her hand, full of the abominations and filthiness of her fornication." (*Rev.* 17:4) It would be no stretch to equate this cup with the Holy Grail, a traditional symbol of the bloodline of Christ, and of the

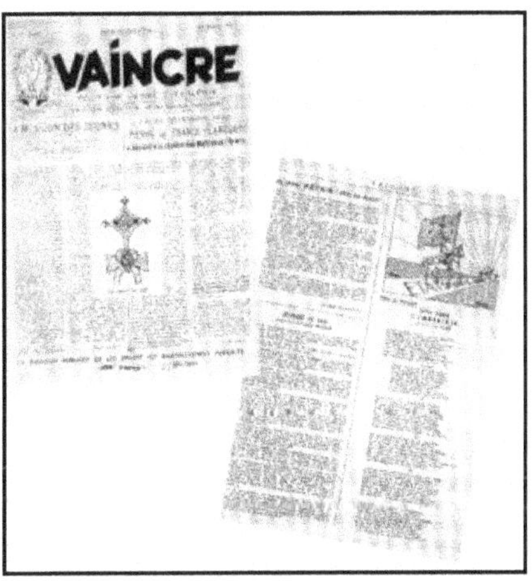
VAINCRE

womb that bore his descendants - the womb of Mary Magdalen (whose name, "Magdol" in the Babylonian tongue, means "Tower", as in the "Tower of Babel.") She too is traditionally thought of as a whore, and is worshipped in Southern France as an incarnation of Ishtar, in the form of the "Black Madonna." She also is depicted in Catholic iconography as holding a vase, "filled with healing balm", as it says in the poem *Le Serpent Rouge*, which she used to anoint Christ as the King of Judah just prior to his crucifixion. And we know that the "filthiness of her fornication" with Jesus is what beget the Merovingian bloodline that shall once more rule the European empire in the coming age.

To be sure, the resurrection of the Holy Roman Empire via the European Union is a stated goal of the modern Merovingian mouthpiece, the Priory of Zion, which has been manipulating European politics behind the scenes for decades now. As early as 1942, the Priory began publicly calling for a "United States of Europe", to be ruled over by kings of Merovingian descent. They even proposed a flag for the new empire, a circle of stars, like those which adorn the crown of the Queen of Heaven, and which adorn the flag of the EU today. An illustration from the Priory's official publication, *Vaincre*, depicts a woman, presumably Europa, holding this flag and riding towards a sunset that is marked with the astrological sign of Aquarius, and mounted upon a white horse.

"A pale horse", you say?

Interestingly, although supposedly at odds with orthodox Catholicism because of their claim to be descendants of Christ, and to be in possession of his "true teachings", the Priory is also known under the official subtitle, "C.I.R.C.U.I.T." - an acronym for French words which translate to, "Chivalry of Catholic Rules and Institutions of the Independent and Traditionalist Union." It is easy to see how the Catholic church could be "reformed" by descendants of Christ, armed with his as-yet-unrevealed teachings, and formed into a true "Universal Church" that could assimilate Protestants, Jews, and even pagans. This could then be used as the theological basis for a revised Holy Roman Empire, ruled by an emperor with descent from Christ, King David, and Cain, making him acceptable to all three religious groups, a Messiah to all cultures, ushering in an era of spiritual revival and global unity. He may even function as a priest-king, and because of his lineage, might be worshipped as an incarnation of God. This all sounds, to Bible prophecy preachers, a heck of a lot like the Anti-Christ. The "False Prophet" who initiates the worship of the Anti-Christ, described in Revelation as a beast with "two horns like a lamb", may be the Pope, who wears a miter with two horns - which, by the way, is modeled after a hat that was traditionally worn by Nimrod.

In addition to the European empire, the Merovingian descendants also covet the throne of Jerusalem, which is rightfully theirs through Davidic (and Messianic) descent. Through their military arm, the Knights Templar, the Priory of Zion initiated the Crusades to capture Jerusalem from the Saracens, and make it a part of the Holy Roman Empire. The Templars were chartered, and hosted their headquarters on the Temple Mount itself, by Merovingian descendant Baldwin I, who held the title "King of Jerusalem." This title is held today by Merovingian descendant Otto von Hapsburg of Austria, a member of the dynasty that last held the throne of the Holy Roman Empire. The Crusaders ultimately lost the Holy Land, which remained under Muslim influence until Britain (Israelite descendants) and the World Zionist Congress created the modern state of Israel, a homeland for apostate Jews which officially came into existence in 1948 with the assistance of military might. This was one of the major signs of the coming of the Apocalypse, according to Bible prophecy preachers, laying the groundwork for the creation of the "New Jerusalem." Since that time, there has been nothing but conflict between the occupying Jewish settlers and the uprooted Palestinians, a group named after the Bible's accursed "Philistines", who worshipped Cain in the form of the fish-god, Dagon. This conflict threatens now more than ever to erupt into a massive world war between the Islamic East and the Occident, a conflict that could result in the Final Battle of Armageddon predicted at the Apocalypse. Another great sign of the End Times will be the re-building of the Temple of Jerusalem, and the erection of the "Abomination of Desolation", an idol of the Anti-Christ to which sacrifices will be made within the temple's inner sanctum. Interestingly, some have claimed that this is already in the works. Guy Patton reports in his book, *Web of Gold* that: "Rabbi Ariel Bar Tzadok, and expert in the Torah and cabalistic prophecy, reported in 1997 that a cornerstone for the future third temple has already been laid less than 50 metres from the mosque at the centre of the Temple Mount." Patton believes that if any of the lost treasures of Solomon's Temple were to be discovered and publicly revealed, "the effect on the Jewish communities in Jerusalem, and elsewhere, would be dramatic, almost certainly resulting in a call from the Orthodox to rebuild the great Temple..." The Priory of Zion has publicly announced that they have possession of these items. And although they have yet to be revealed, something of a temple reconstruction did take place on April 18, 2001, when, as David Hatcher Childress writes, "Israel unveiled the 'Virtual Temple', a computer replica of the ancient temple and what it was like to visit the holy sanctuary." The press release put out for the event reports that: "The computer simulation is just part of a new interactive museum that opened Wednesday just outside the Al Asqa Mosque, which sits on the land where Jews believe the remains of their two temples - one built by King Solomon, and the second, by King Herod - are buried..." This rebuilding of the

Temple appears to be part of a plot, not only by the Jews, but also on the part of the Vatican, which appears to be commencing an effort to unite with Judaism and form a true one-world religion. Writes Tim Cohen in *The Anti-Christ and a Cup of Tea*: "In September, 1993, [Shimon] Peres signed a secret deal with the Pope promising Vatican hegemony over Jerusalem's Old City by the year 2000." Peres' friend Mark Halter, who was apparently in charge of delivering the message to the Pope, was quoted as saying that, "The city will stay the capital of Israel, but will be administered by the Vatican. The city will have an Israeli mayor and a Palestinian mayor, both under orders from the Holy See." A few yeas later, the Pope, barely able to stand, made the difficult journey to Jerusalem to make a formal reconciliation with the Jewish nation, apologizing for the Vatican's seeming complicity with the Nazis during the Holocaust. And on March 11, 2001, Israeli President Moshe Katsav was named by the *Bild* newspaper as saying that he was "firmly in favor of his country joining the European Union." One can see the above-mentioned actions initiating a backlash from the entire Muslim world that could result in the prophesized Battle of Armageddon.

But is the Bible being literal when it speaks of the Anti-Christ as a "king" who will sit on the throne of David, or will he be a mere "President" or "Prime Minister"? Tim Cohen, who believes that the Merovingian descendant Prince Charles of England is the Anti-Christ, claims that the Prince (who, by the way, has been asked to be called "Defender of *All* Faiths", instead of the traditional "Defender of the Faith" when he assumes the throne of England) has put in a formal request to become the King of the European Union as well. But monarchy is an anachronism of the past, is it not? Indeed, both patriotism and religious faith were thought of as anachronisms before September 11. Now they are back with fury. How far away is a revitalization of the monarchical system? The United States has even favored the return of Afghanistan's former king, Mohammed Zahir Shah, after the dismantling of the Taliban regime. And of course, it is hard not to notice that our current President did not win his office by popular vote, but by a twist of fate that allowed him to assume the "throne" once occupied by his father, President Bush Sr, the equivalent of a monarchial succession. He even appears to be carrying on with the work of his predecessor, fighting a continuation of his father's battle with the Islamic world, complete with many of the same cabinet members. But unlike his father, Bush Jr. has achieved an unprecedented unification of the public behind himself and his agenda, and acquired a loyalty from the populace not seen since the institution of representational government replaced that of monarchy. Bush even sees his "reign" in messianic terms, and has been quoted as saying that he believes himself to be on a "divine mission." He speaks of our enemies as "evildoers", and of the current war against them as a new "crusade" - rather like the ones initiated by the his ancestors, the Knights Templar. Indeed, we do have a home-grown royal family, and it's not the Kennedy's, but the Bush's - a royal family that intends to lead us into the New World Order (George Sr.'s terminology), and the Final Battle of Armageddon. Even Ronald Reagan, who preceded George Bush Sr. in the White House, has been quoted as saying during his Presidential campaign that, "I sometimes believe we're headed very fast for Armageddon right now."

So the men in charge of the Western World, who have the power to manipulate the world events that would make Armageddon possible are aware that the prophecies of the End Times are being fulfilled, and they are doing nothing to stop it, but in fact are working to bring them to fruition. Could it be that they are consciously fulfilling what they see as their apocalyptic destiny, and are purposely going about steps to hasten the rise of the Anti-Christ? Are the leaders of the Western world willingly serving the powers of evil?

Perhaps. We know that the Merovingian kings are associated with a bloodline that has long practiced religious rites absolutely forbidden to the Israelites by their god, but which nonetheless captured the allegiance of many of their kings. We know that these religious rites are still practiced today by the secret societies to which many of our leaders belong, and that these leaders come from this bloodline as well. We know that this bloodline, although it includes Jesus Christ, ultimately stems from Cain, who was believed by the Israelites to have been cursed, the son of the Devil himself. And this is also a trait that the prophecies say will be shared by the Anti-Christ. The Mark of Cain, which God placed upon his forehead as a seal of protection against the vengeful tendencies of his countrymen, may be the equivalent of the Mark of the Beast, which the Anti-Christ will one day force his subjects to be branded with. From an Orthodox Christian perspective, any global government set up by such a person would be the Kingdom of Satan, and any religious images that he might have erected in a newly-rebuilt Temple of Solomon would be called the "Abomination of Desolation."

But perhaps it is more complicated than that. Evidence indicates that these Merovingian descendants see themselves as fulfilling a cosmic destiny that is beyond good and evil. To them, fulfilling one's pre-ordained role in history is a sacred duty, whether for good or for evil, and that end justifies any means. This is one of the most basic and universal tenets of the secret societies and mystery schools to which our global leaders belong. In fact, achieving a balance of good and evil energies is one of their most treasured secrets, and they seek to embody that principle in everything they do. They see the Devil as a brother of Christ, and some even see that Anti-Christ as a sort of "second Messiah." There is even a Koranic tradition that there will be two messiahs at the End Times, the "Messiah ben David", and his arch-rival, the "Messiah ben Joseph." Since the appearance of both messiahs is necessary in order for the return of the Kingdom of God to ensue, those who bring about the rise of the "Anti-Christ" figure are actually playing a vital role in God's plan.

This, it appears, is what the members of the "Bloodline of the Holy Grail" have set about to do, and it certainly does not appear that they intend to sit back and let destiny unroll before them like a carpet. They actively work, plot, and conspire to actualize their prophesized destiny. Evidence indicates that Jesus Christ conspired with others to fulfill the traditional messianic prophecies of his culture, and actually became the Messiah by means of his action and will. This concept was explored in the 1960s with the publication of Dr. Hugh Schonfield's *The Passover Plot,* and is a major component of the theory that Christ faked his death on the cross so that he could go on to father a royal dynasty in France. Might not his descendants now be enacting an "Apocalypse Plot" in order to hasten the return of God's kingdom on Earth? They also see themselves as descendants of Cain, destined to being about a new "Golden Age", with a global empire much like that which existed during his reign. Eastern tradition says that every new age is opened by an "avatar", an incarnation of the "Lord of the Earth" (one of the titles used by Cain), who overthrows the old order and institutes a new order throughout the world. Since the prevailing order today is mainly Judeo-Christian, any avatar of a new age would be perceived by adherents of the old order as necessarily "Anti-Christian", even if he is of the same bloodline as the previous avatar, Christ. Indeed, throughout history, kings have most often had their kingdoms overthrown by their own children. Orthodox Christians might find it a sickening irony that the Anti-Christ would actually be one of Christ's descendants, but to the servants of the Holy Grail, it is seen as poetic and pre-ordained. They also understand the necessity of Apocalypse in between ages, to cleanse the Earth of anything that is unfit to exist within the new paradigm. This is the burden of destiny that the members of the Grail family have evidently taken upon themselves, and they stand poised to lead us into a golden sunset marked, as it is in the *Vaincre* illustration, with the sign of the Age of Aquarius.

It is the Age of Aquarius which our globe is currently heading into, the sign of the water-bearer, fresh on the heals of the previous age of Pisces, the fishes, another water sign. This, according to many interpreters, signifies that the previous age from which we are just emerging was dominated by Christian ideology, since Christ's major symbol (prior to the imposition of the paganized cross as his symbol) was the "Ichthys" fish sign. But why are there two fish in the zodiac sign of Pisces? If Christ was one of the fish, who is the

other? An interesting interpretation can be found in C.G. Jung's *Aion,* in a chapter called "The Ambivalence of the Fish Symbol." In it he explores Jewish cabalistic traditions which state that: "The time preceding the coming of the Messiah falls in twelve parts, and the Messiah will appear in the twelfth. As a time division, the number twelve points to the Zodia, of which the twelfth is the Fishes. Leviathan will then rise out of the sea." Jung argues that the Pisces were originally not mere fishes, but the two sea-monsters mentioned in the Bible, Behemoth and Leviathan. These two beasts, eternally locked in conflict, represent, he says, the Lord Yahweh struggling with his split-off shadow self, the Devil. They also symbolically allude to Christ and his twin brother, the Anti-Christ. These two shall fight one final battle, equivalent to battle of Gog and Magog mentioned in *Revelation*, says Jung. Afterwards, apocryphal tradition teaches that Leviathan will be cut up and served as Eucharistic food to the righteous few who survive the Tribulation. This symbolizes the end of the Age of Pisces, and any kingdom that would be established afterwards would rule during the Age of Aquarius.

The importance of all this fish and water symbolism should be obvious to any *Dagobert's Revenge* reader. For as we have argued numerous times before, the messianic Merovingian bloodline descends not only from Christ the fish, and the Judeo-Christian line of David, but also from the Tribe of Dan, the Philistines, the Canaanites, the Phoenicians, the Babylonians, the Sumerians, and ultimately, the Atlanteans, whose world-famous monarch, Cain, "the Quinotaur", is the Merovingians' most celebrated ancestor. All of these groups were known in their times as "sea peoples", who had built their empires largely with their mastery of the skills of navigation. Also, Cain, as you will recall, was the inspiration for the legendary figure of Leviathan. Cain's glorious Atlantean empire was destroyed in the previous apocalypse, and sank beneath the salty green waves of the sea. But the stated goal of Cain's Merovingian descendants, and the current world leaders who serve them, is to build a new Atlantis, and this resurrection is often pictured as actually involving the continent of Atlantis itself literally rising up out of the sea - sort of like Leviathan is prophesized to rise out of the sea at the end of the world. Perhaps this prophecy merely symbolizes the rising global empire that the Merovingians are bringing to fruition right now. Such an unbridled beast will need to be reigned in by a strong master, a messianic king who will "rule the nations with an iron scepter", and hold dominion over the Earth. God willing, you and I will be among the lucky few to witness this unveiling of the ages, the crowning glory of the generations. ‡

Gustave Dore's, The Death of Abel

Dagobert's Revenge
PO BOX 18331
DENVER, CO 80218-0331
USA

www.ingramcontent.com/pod-product-compliance
Lightning Source LLC
Chambersburg PA
CBHW050442200726
48295CB00024B/942

* 9 7 8 1 9 6 2 3 1 2 2 1 9 *